# CHARLIE BROWN'S 'CYCLOPEDIA

### Super Questions and Answers and Amazing Facts

## Featuring The Earth, Weather and Climate

## Volume 9

### Based on the Charles M. Schulz Characters

Funk & Wagnalls, Inc.

Photograph and Illustration Credits: The Bettmann Archive, Inc., xi.

A large part of this volume was previously published in *Charlie Brown's Second Super Book of Questions and Answers.*

# Introduction

Welcome to volume 9 of *Charlie Brown's 'Cyclopedia*! Have you ever wondered why the ocean is salty, or how the mountains were made, or what makes the winds blow? Charlie Brown and the rest of the *Peanuts* gang are here to help you find the answers to these questions and many more about the earth, weather, and climate. Have fun!

# The Earth

## What is the earth made of?

The earth is a great ball of rock. Underneath its grass, soil, oceans, and rivers lie thousands of miles of rock.

If you could dig a hole deep into the earth, here is what you would find. At first you would see hard rock, like the kind you see above ground. The rock would feel cool when you touched it. This rock is part of the crust, or outside, of the earth. As you went deeper, the crust would become hotter and hotter. When you got about 5 miles (8 kilometers) into the earth's rock it would be hot enough to roast you alive! If you could keep digging in spite of this heat, you would reach the part of the earth called the mantle. This starts about 20 miles (32 kilometers) below the ground. Most of the rock here would be hard. But some would be soft and gluey—like very thick molasses. And the temperature would still be rising. The center, or core, of the earth may be as hot as nine thousand degrees Fahrenheit (9,000° F., or 5,000° C.)! A lot of this core is liquid rock.

No one has ever dug far enough to see or feel what the earth is like deep inside. However, scientists have machines that can gather information without ever going below the ground.

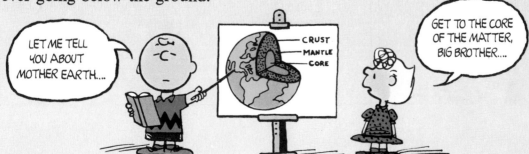

385

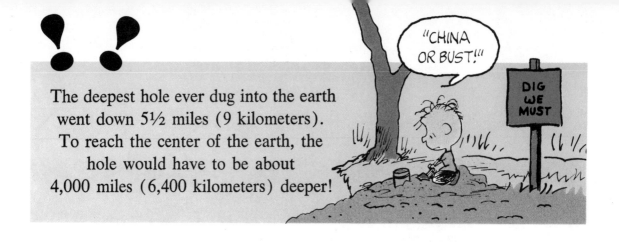

The deepest hole ever dug into the earth went down 5½ miles (9 kilometers). To reach the center of the earth, the hole would have to be about 4,000 miles (6,400 kilometers) deeper!

## Why is the inside of the earth hot?

Many scientists believe that billions of years ago the earth was a great ball of dust and gas. Over a long period of time, the bits of dust and gas moved closer and closer together. Finally, they joined to become solid rock. All the movement caused by the shrinking made the earth heat up. In fact, it got so hot that the rock melted into a gluey liquid. After millions of years, the outside of the earth—the crust—cooled off. Because it cooled, it became hard rock again—in the same way that melted chocolate gets hard when it cools in the refrigerator. But the inside of the earth did not cool. It has stayed hot until today because certain minerals in the earth give off a lot of energy and heat. We say that these minerals are radioactive (RAY-dee-oh-AK-tiv).

# Does hot rock ever come out of the earth?

Yes. Hot, liquid rock called lava comes out of volcanoes. Scientists give the name "volcano" to any crack in the earth's crust from which lava flows.

Scientists are not sure what makes a volcano act up—or erupt. But they think that hot gases inside the earth push lava up from below. The force of these gases may also cause the loud noise that people sometimes hear when a volcano erupts.

The earth may shake when a volcano erupts. Out comes fiery-hot, glowing lava. Steam, ashes, and even solid rocks pour out, too. Once the lava reaches the surface of the earth, it cools and hardens. Often so much lava, rock, and ash come out that a mountain builds up around the crack. Then the whole mountain, with its crack, is called a volcano. A big volcano mountain can take as long as ten thousand years to build up. But one volcano in Mexico grew 200 feet (60 meters) high in a single day.

No volcano keeps erupting all the time. The rest period of a volcano may be just a few minutes, a few months, a few years, or several hundred years. And some volcanoes stop erupting altogether. We say these volcanoes are extinct.

IT SAYS HERE SCIENTISTS ARE NOT SURE WHAT MAKES A VOLCANO ERUPT.... WHICH REMINDS ME A LOT OF MY SISTER.

VERY FUNNY... OH, VERY FUNNY!!!

VOLCANOES ARE LITTER BUGS

A Hawaiian volcano once threw out a block of stone that weighed at much as four big trucks. The stone landed half a mile (almost a kilometer) away!

## Are volcanoes dangerous?

Yes. The hot lava that pours out of a volcano often causes fires. Sometimes so much lava flows that it buries a whole city or a whole island. Also, when a volcano erupts, it often sends out a cloud of smoke filled with poisonous gases. The gases spread over a large area and kill everyone who breathes them in.

Volcanoes are most dangerous on islands. Because islands are surrounded by water, people have a hard time escaping.

## Do volcanoes do any good?

Yes. The inside of a volcano is very, very hot. It heats everything around it, too. At several places in the world, people have learned to use this heat.

Much of the earth's water is underground. The underground water around an active volcano—one that erupts from time to time—is very hot. Wells have been drilled near such volcanoes. Pipes have been put down the wells, deep enough to reach the boiling-hot underground water. Up through the pipes has come steam given off by the boiling water. The steam is used to turn machines that make electricity.

The greatest gift of volcanoes is their help in making rich soil. All soil is made mostly of crumbled rock. Soil made from volcanic rock has in it many of the minerals that help plants to grow well. The land around a volcano is the best farmland in the world. However, farmers must live with the knowledge that the volcano may erupt again at any time.

## What is a hot spring?

Some parts of the earth have natural hot or warm water under the ground. If this water comes up above the ground through a crack, people call it a hot spring.

Some hot springs are hot because their water comes from far down in the earth where there is great heat. But the water from most hot springs starts closer to the top of the earth. This water is hot because it is near a volcano. The volcano may be an active one, or it may be one that is extinct.

## What is Old Faithful?

Old Faithful is a geyser (GUY-zur) in Yellowstone National Park, Wyoming. A geyser is a special kind of hot spring. Its water gets so hot underground that it boils and explodes into steam. The geyser spurts the hot water and steam into the air from an opening in the ground. The water shoots up like a fountain for a while, and then dies down. The water in some geysers rises only a couple of inches. In others, it shoots as high as a ten-story building. Some geysers spurt only once every few years. Old Faithful got its name by shooting water faithfully about once every hour. It shoots the water as high as a seven-story building. Old Faithful's water is hot because about a million years ago small volcanoes existed in the Yellowstone area.

389

## What is an earthquake?

Any snapping or breaking of the earth's crust is called an earthquake. The snapping makes the earth shake, or quake. If you were to snap a plastic ruler in two, you would see the two halves shaking for a few seconds after the snap. That is what happens to the earth during an earthquake. But in the earth, the shaking lasts longer than a few seconds.

Forces inside the earth are always squeezing and straining the rock of the earth's crust. Scientists aren't sure why this happens. Usually the forces cause the rock to bend, but not snap. So there is no earthquake. But sometimes the forces are so great that they make the rock snap. If you are close to where the rock has snapped, you feel the earth shiver. You feel the earthquake.

## Can an earthquake change the surface of the earth?

Yes. A big earthquake can break off part of a mountain, which then tumbles down onto the land below it. An earthquake can tear open the ground. It can shove huge blocks of land around. Any of these things can happen in just a few minutes.

Big earthquakes cause a lot of damage. Buildings fall down. Gas pipes burst and start fires. Whole cities sometimes start burning. Water pipes break, so there is no water to put out the fires. Many people are killed by the falling buildings or the fire. Luckily, most earthquakes are small. They do very little damage.

In the year 1556, about 830,000 people died in one earthquake in China!

# How can you protect yourself from earthquakes?

The best way to protect yourself from earthquakes is to stay away from the areas where they happen. Earthquakes do not happen in all parts of the world. They happen in special areas called earthquake belts. One runs along the western coasts of North and South America.

If you *do* live in an earthquake belt, it helps to live in a well-built house with a steel frame. The house should be built on solid rock—not on soft clay. If an earthquake does begin, don't panic. Don't rush out into the street. People have been trampled to death during earthquakes by crowds of panicky people in the streets.

Today, scientists have machines that measure the movements in the earth. They can sometimes tell when an earthquake is coming, so that people can get out of an area before the quake starts.

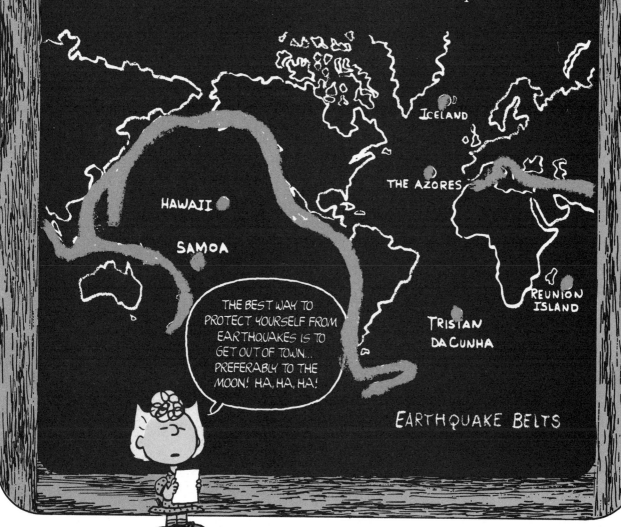

## What is a fossil?

A fossil is the remains of a plant or an animal that lived millions of years ago. Some fossils are shells and bones of animals that have turned to stone. Some are leaf prints left in rock. Others are tracks of animals, such as dinosaurs, that hardened into stone. These tracks look like footsteps made in cement.

## How were the mountains made?

Many mountains were made from rock that was pushed up from the bottom of the ocean. Scientists know this because fossils of ancient sea animals are buried in the tops of the highest mountains.

Mud and sand—called sediment (SED-uh-mint)—are always being carried by rivers from the land down into the ocean. Sediment that was carried to the ocean many millions of years ago came to rest in low places on the ocean floor. The skeletons of sea animals became mixed with the sediment. For hundreds of thousands of years, sediment piled up in layers on the ocean floor. The sand, mud, and skeletons got packed and squeezed together into solid rock. After many more thousands of years, forces inside the earth squeezed the rock into folds—the way you can squeeze the skin on the back of your hand into folds with your thumb and another finger. Finally, these forces pushed the folded rock upward to make many of the mountains we see today.

Rock is pushed up into mountains.

Layers are squeezed into folds.

# How many different kinds of rock are there?

There are three groups of rock. All the rocks you can ever find belong to one of these three groups.

The first group is called igneous (IG-nee-us) rock. It started out deep under the ground. At one time it was so hot that it was a gluey liquid. Most igneous rock cooled and hardened underneath the earth. But some of the liquid—lava —broke through to the earth's surface. It flowed out from volcanoes, and then hardened. One type of igneous rock, granite, is often used for statues and build- ings because it is very strong.

The second group of rock was made from sand, mud, or clay that rivers washed down from the land into the sea. It was packed down on the ocean floor in layers. Later, much of this rock rose again to make mountains. This kind of rock is called sedimentary (sed-uh-MEN-tuh-ree) rock. Cement is made from a sedimentary rock called limestone.

The third kind of rock is one that was once either igneous or sedimentary rock. But for millions of years it was bent, folded, twisted, squeezed, and heated by forces in the earth. And so it was changed into a different kind of rock. This kind is called metamorphic (met-uh-MORE-fik) rock, which means "rock that has been changed." The "lead" in a pencil is really graphite, which comes from a metamorphic rock.

WOW, HERE'S A BEAUTY FOR MY ROCK COLLECTION.

I FOUND ONE! I FOUND ONE! I FOUND A—ER— IGNEOUS ROCK!

PAY ATTENTION, SCOUTS, AND REPEAT AFTER ME: "IGNEOUS, SEDIMENTARY, METAMORPHIC." I DIDN'T WIN MY EAGLE BADGE FOR NOTHING, YOU KNOW!

> **!** Most rock is very hard and stiff. But itacolumite (it-uh-KOL-yuh-mite) **!**
> is so flexible, you can bend it with your two hands!

# What are rocks made of?

All rocks are made of one or more minerals. If you look closely at most rocks, you will see speckles in them. These speckles are minerals. You can see some of them shine if you hold the rocks in bright light. The size, shape, and pattern of the minerals can help you figure out what kind of rocks you're looking at.

There are about 2,500 known minerals in the world. They have different colors, feel different to the touch, and have different strengths. But all of them are made of pieces called crystals. Minerals are found only in nature. They are never man-made. Some minerals you may know are quartz, copper, gold, and diamonds.

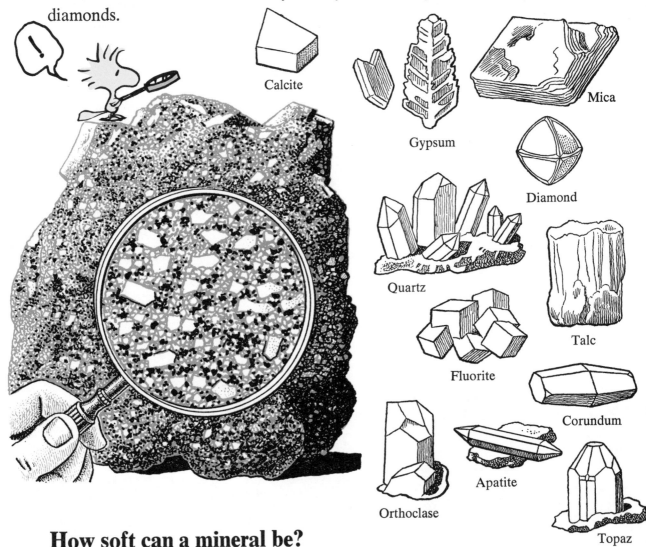

Calcite

Gypsum

Mica

Diamond

Quartz

Talc

Fluorite

Corundum

Apatite

Orthoclase

Topaz

# How soft can a mineral be?

A mineral can be soft enough to be scratched by your fingernail. This means that your fingernail is harder than the mineral. Talc is one of these very soft minerals. It is so soft, in fact, that baby powder is made from it! Most minerals, however, are harder—some a lot harder and some just a little.

# What is the hardest mineral?

A diamond is the hardest of all minerals. The only thing that can scratch a diamond is another diamond. Because diamonds are so rare and hard and beautiful, they are very valuable and are used to make rings and other jewelry.

# How do people get minerals out of the earth?

People get useful minerals such as tin and copper out of the ground by mining. Most minerals are not easy to get out of the earth. Miners tear them out with picks and shovels. Sometimes miners have to drill the minerals out of the earth, or blast them out with explosives such as dynamite.

## Is all mining done underground?

No. When people mine a mineral that lies near the top of the earth, they don't have to dig underground. To get at the mineral, miners can just strip off a thin layer of soil with machines, such as bulldozers. This kind of mining is easier and faster than mining far underneath the ground. No long holes and tunnels have to be dug. However, miners have ruined the land in some places by mining from the top. They have not put the soil back where it belongs so that plants can grow there again.

GOOD GRIEF

I FOUND THREE PENNIES HERE TODAY. I BET THERE'S A COPPER MINE BURIED UNDER THE GROUND.

## Is coal made of minerals?

No. Coal is made of the remains of plants that lived many millions of years ago. At that time much of the earth's land was flat and swampy. In the swamps grew huge forests of ferns, mosses, and large trees. As the plants died, they fell into the swamps and began to rot. New plants grew over them. Then they died and new plants grew over them. This happened over and over. Finally, the top layers of dead plants packed and squeezed those at the bottom into a spongy material called peat.

After millions of more years, the swampy land sank in many areas. Water ran into the low places. Mud and sand were washed into the water and covered the peat. The weight of the mud and sand packed and squeezed the peat even more. The peat became buried inside the earth, where it was very hot. The heat, together with the heavy weight, finally turned the peat into hard, black coal.

# Did cave men make caves?

No, cave men didn't make caves. They found the caves and lived in them because they had no other homes.

Most really big caves are made of a soft rock called limestone. For thousands of years, rain water kept dripping down through tiny holes in this rock. Very slowly, the water wore away the rock, forming hollow caves.

At first, caves are filled with water. But over a long period, most of the water runs out.

# What are the stone "icicles" found inside many caves?

Water runs along the ceiling of a limestone cave, picking up bits of a mineral called calcite (KAL-site) that is in the limestone. Some of the water goes up into the air—evaporates. But the calcite does not. So it is left on the ceiling. As more water evaporates, more of the calcite is left on the ceiling. It begins to form a bump. Slowly, more and more water runs over the bump and drips downward. The bump grows down from the ceiling like an icicle. It is called a stalactite (stuh-LAK-tite).

Water that drips to the floor of the cave also evaporates. The calcite from the water builds up on the floor. The calcite forms what looks like an upside-down icicle. This is called a stalagmite (stuh-LAG-mite). Sometimes a stalagmite grows up until it joins a stalactite that is growing down. Together they form a long column from the floor to the ceiling.

The longest known stalactite is in Spain.
It is 195 feet (59 meters) long.
That's about the size of 32 tall men
standing on each other's shoulders!

## What is soil?

Soil is the dark-brown covering over most land. It can be a few inches or a few feet thick. Some people call soil "dirt."

Soil is made mostly of tiny bits of rock of different sizes. It also has in it tiny pieces of plants and animals that have died. Mixed in with soil, too, are tiny living things such as bacteria (back-TEER-ee-uh)—germs so small you need a microscope to see them. Soil also has water and air in it.

## How was soil formed?

Billions of years ago, when the earth was young, there was no soil. Only water and rock lay on the surface of the earth. Rain and wind began to beat against the rock. Swift rivers and ocean waves pounded at the rocks. Slowly they wore the rock down. Water seeped into cracks in the rock. In cold weather, the water froze. Frozen water—ice—takes up more space than liquid water. So the ice pushed against both sides of a crack. It split the rock into stones. Rain and rivers washed the stones down rocky mountains and wore them down into smaller rocks and pebbles. After millions of years, a layer of very tiny pieces of rock built up on top of the earth. Pieces of dead plants and animals got mixed in with the bits of rock. This mixture is soil.

## What is clay?

Clay is a special kind of soil. It is made up of fine bits—grains—of rock, tinier than those in most other kinds of soil. Many of the grains are bits of certain minerals called clay minerals. Kaolinite (KAY-uh-luh-nite) is the most common one. Clay minerals cause the clay grains to pack together tightly so they can be molded into any shape at all. When clay is baked, it gets hard. So clay is used to make bricks, pots, dishes, and other useful things.

# How many oceans are there in the world?

Even though we talk about the Atlantic Ocean, the Pacific Ocean, and others, there is really just one ocean. Make a small paper boat and then try sailing it around the globe in your classroom. Start the boat at any point in the ocean. Keep it going in the water. Can you find a place where your boat must stop sailing? No. That's because all the oceans of the world are really one big ocean. Somewhere in each "ocean" there is a place where the water is joined to the water of another "ocean." The ocean has no end.

## How was the ocean formed?

The earth did not always have a great ocean, as it does today. Many millions of years ago, the earth was very hot. Some scientists believe that at that time, most of the earth's water was trapped deep inside its rocks. Over millions of years, the rocks began to cool and harden. As they got hard, their water came out. It ran into the low places in the earth's crust and made the first oceans. Other scientists think the water came from great clouds that were all around the earth. As the hot earth cooled, the clouds cooled, too. Clouds that get cooler form raindrops. So the clouds around the earth rained for hundreds of years, filling the earth's low places.

Since then, the number, shape, and size of the oceans have changed. But an ocean is still a large, low area filled with water.

# Where is the deepest part of the ocean?

The deepest spot is in the Pacific Ocean, near the Mariana Islands. Here the water is over 36,000 feet (10,900 meters) deep—or nearly 7 miles (11 kilometers) from the surface to the bottom. This is deep enough to swallow the highest mountain in the world—Mount Everest—which is nearly 6 miles (10 kilometers) high.

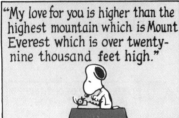

 If you were to drop a rock the size of your head into water 36,000 feet (10,900 meters) deep, it would take the rock about an hour to reach the bottom!

# Why is the ocean salty?

The ocean tastes salty because there's a lot of salt in it. Most of this salt came from the land. Salt is a mineral that can be found in many rocks and in soil, too. When rain falls on the earth, some of it soaks into the ground. Some of it also trickles over rocks and along the soil. The flowing water picks up some salt and carries it to rivers. Rivers flow into the ocean. And with them goes a little salt. Because this has happened for millions of years, the ocean now has a great deal of salt in it. Rivers are far less salty, because they keep dumping their salt into the ocean—where it stays.

401

Water samples taken from the ocean at opposite ends
of the world have the same amount of salt in them!

## What is a salt lick?

A salt lick is a chunk of rock salt that animals like to lick. Salt is found in large rocky "beds," or layers, in the ground. These layers are made up of tiny salt grains packed tightly together so that they form rock. Long, long ago, salty ocean water lay where the salt beds are now. But the water dried up and left the salt. In a few places, part of a salt bed will stick out of the top of the earth. Such bare rocks of salt are called salt licks. Animals come there to lick salt because their bodies need it. Sometimes farmers put a chunk of rock salt in a cow pasture. This chunk is also called a salt lick.

# What are tides?

Did you ever sit on a sandy beach and watch the ocean water move closer and closer to you? If you did, you were watching the tide come in. If you were still on the beach later that day, you saw the tide go out again. That means that the ocean water moved back. Once again you could see the sand that the water had covered.

In most places in the world, tides go in and out this way twice each day. They do so because the ocean water rises and falls. The rise and fall are caused by gravity—the great invisible force that all stars, planets, and moons have. The force of gravity pulls things toward the center of the star, planet, or moon. The gravity of the sun and the gravity of the moon both pull on the earth's ocean water, causing tides. The moon is much nearer the earth than the sun. So the moon's pull on the ocean water is the stronger one. Of course, the moon pulls on the earth's land as well. But the land is solid. The moon's pull isn't strong enough to move it much. Ocean water is liquid, and so it moves a lot when the moon's gravity pulls on it.

## Do lakes and rivers have tides?

Yes, they do. But their tides are usually too small to be noticed.

# What makes waves in the ocean?

Waves are ridges, or swells, of water on top of the ocean. They travel one after another across the sea. Most waves are caused by wind blowing over the top of the water. When wind begins to blow over a smooth stretch of water, it makes little ripples. If the wind keeps on blowing in the same direction, the ripples grow bigger. They get to be waves. The longer and harder the wind blows, the bigger the waves get.

# What is a tidal wave?

A tidal wave has nothing to do with tides. It is a gigantic wave caused by an earthquake under the ocean. The quake pushes a part of the sea floor up or down and starts a long wave. The wave travels very fast, sometimes hundreds of miles an hour. As it travels it grows. At first, a tidal wave may be only a few feet high. But by the time it reaches land, the water has piled up much higher. A tidal wave can grow to be 100 feet (30 meters) high. When it hits the shore, it causes great damage. Today scientists all over the world call a tidal wave by its Japanese name—tsunami (tsoo-NAH-mee).

405

## Where do rivers come from?

Rivers start with rain. Wherever rain falls or snow melts, some water flows downhill. No place on the earth is perfectly level, or flat. There is always a little slope. Water moves down the slope toward the lowest place. The flowing water carves out ditches in the ground. With every new rainfall, the ditches get deeper and wider. They become streams, which flow into other streams. They grow bigger and bigger until they become rivers that flow all the time. Rivers keep flowing until they pour into the ocean.

The Nile River in Africa is more than 4,000 miles (6,400 kilometers) long. That's a lot longer than the distance across the United States from Maine to California!

## What is a glacier?

A glacier (GLAY-shur) is a huge heap of ice and snow so heavy that its own weight moves it downhill. Sometimes glaciers are called "rivers of ice." Like rivers, they keep moving downhill until they reach the ocean—unless they melt first. Glaciers move very slowly. Small ones may move only an inch or so a day. Large glaciers may move as much as 10 feet (3 meters) per day.

## Where do glaciers come from?

In some parts of the world, a lot of snow falls. If the temperature never gets warm enough for all of this snow to melt, new snow piles up on top of old snow. As years go by, the growing heap of snow gets thicker and heavier. Gradually most of it gets packed down into ice. When the heap gets very, very heavy, it begins to slide downhill. It becomes a moving glacier.

## What is an iceberg?

An iceberg is a mountain of ice floating in the sea. It was once part of a glacier. But it broke off when the glacier reached the edge of the ocean. Although the ocean is salty, the ice of an iceberg has no salt in it. An iceberg is made of fresh water that comes from the glacier.

An iceberg is born in a very cold place. It floats out to a warmer area where it begins to melt. For about three years, it keeps traveling and melting little by little. Eventually, it gets very soft, breaks into pieces, and melts away completely.

Some icebergs are about as long as a football field. Others can be as long as 2,900 football fields lined up in a row. Most of an iceberg's ice is hidden underneath the water. What people see is just the tip of the ice sticking out above the water.

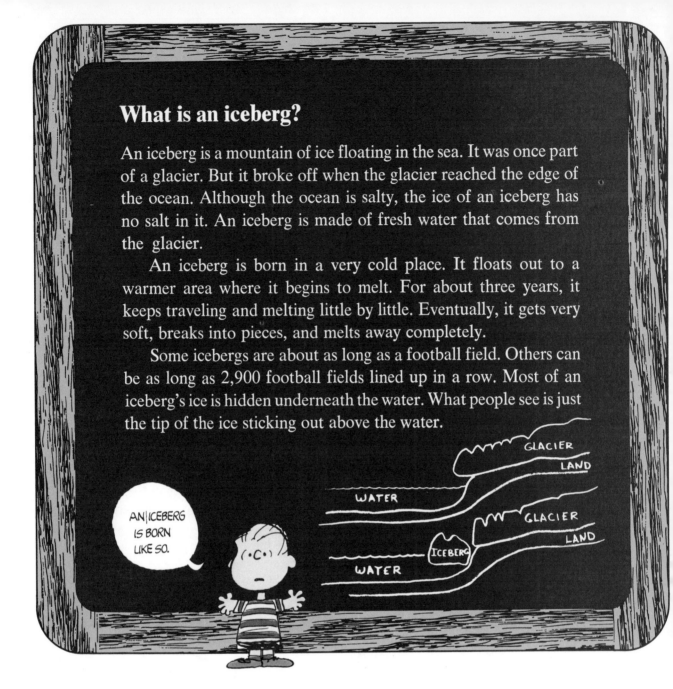

## Why is an iceberg dangerous?

An iceberg is dangerous to ships at sea because it is mostly hidden under water. When a large iceberg is sighted from a ship, no one aboard can tell how far the ice extends under the water. The ship could ram itself on this hidden ice and sink. The only sure way for a ship to be safe from icebergs is to sail away from them.

 An iceberg can weigh a million tons!

# Weather and Climate

## What is weather?

When you talk about weather, you are really talking about the air. Weather is what the air is like in any one place at any one time. How hot or cold is the air? How much dampness, or moisture, is in it? How fast is the air moving? How heavily does it press on the earth? The answers to these questions tell about the weather.

## What's the difference between weather and climate?

Weather tells what the air is like in a place at any one time. Climate tells what the weather is like in general, all year round. If a place has much more dry weather than wet weather, we say it has a dry climate. If it has much more hot weather than cold weather, we say it has a hot climate. Yuma, Arizona, for example, has a hot, dry climate. On most summer, spring, and fall days in Yuma, the weather is dry, sunny, and hot. But on a winter morning, the weather may be rainy and cool. Later that same day, the weather may be dry, sunny, and cool. Weather keeps changing each day. Climate stays much the same one year after another.

409

# How many different climates are there in the world?

Each place in the world has its own climate. But many climates are so much alike that scientists have grouped them all into just twelve types. Each type describes how hot or cold and how dry or wet a place is.

The United States has ten of the twelve types of climate. They range from the climate of Miami to the climate of Alaska. Miami is almost always very warm and is rainy half the year. Parts of Alaska are always cold and fairly dry.

# What makes climates different?

The location of a place on the earth decides its climate. If you live far to the north, where the red arrow is pointing, you live in a cold climate. The same would be true if you lived very far to the south, where the green arrow is pointing. The sun's rays hit these areas at a great slant and don't warm the land very much. But if you live somewhere around the middle of the earth—near what we call the equator (ih-KWAY-tur)—your hometown probably has a climate that is hot all year round. That is because the sun's rays hit this area fairly directly. The more directly the sun's rays hit a place, the warmer that place is. If you live near the equator, your hometown not only gets more sun, but it also gets more rain than places very far north or south.

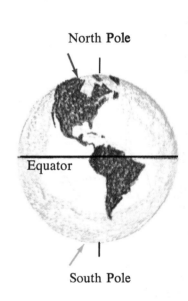

North **Pole**

Equator

South Pole

How high up you live also makes a difference in the climate. If you live in the mountains, you are likely to have a cooler climate than if you lived lower down.

If you live near the ocean, your winters are probably less cold and your summers less hot than those in places far from the ocean. But your hometown usually has more rain than those inland places do. Winds and the movement of water in the ocean near your home help to make the climate the way it is.

IF YOU LIVE AT THE EQUATOR, THE CLIMATE IS HOT.

## Are there really "poles" at the North Pole and South Pole?

No. The picture of a pole labeled "North Pole" is just a joke. There are no poles of that sort marking either the North or the South Pole. The word "pole" here means something very different from "a long, thin stick."

The earth is round like a rubber ball. If you were to stick a long pencil through the center of a ball, one end of the pencil would stick out at each end of the ball. In much the same way, scientists have stuck an imaginary line—instead of a pencil—through the earth. The line is called the earth's axis. It is around this axis that the earth turns. The places where the ends of the axis stick out are the North Pole and the South Pole. Circling the earth halfway between the poles is an imaginary line that we call the equator.

## Are the North Pole and the South Pole exactly alike?

No. The point we call the South Pole is on an ice-covered land. The point we call the North Pole is on an ice-covered sea. Water does not cool off as much as land does. So the North Pole does not get quite as cold in the winter as the South Pole. The North Pole is cold enough for most of us, though. A temperature of 73 degrees below zero has been recorded nearby!

A submarine has sailed right under the ice at the North Pole!

THA
SOME
TO T
ABC

## What does "below zero" mean?

When you talk about "below zero," you are talking about a temperature as measured on a thermometer. One kind of thermometer has a line of liquid that moves up and down a tube. Along the tube are numbers. The space between two numbers is called a degree. By seeing how far up or down the tube the line of liquid has moved, you can tell how hot or cold something is. Thermometers are often used to measure the temperature of the air or of water.

People in the United States most often use a thermometer that was invented by Gabriel Fahrenheit (FAIR-in-hite). On his thermometer when the line of liquid reaches 212 degrees, water boils. It freezes and turns to ice at 32 degrees. We write this temperature as 32°F. The "F." stands for Fahrenheit. On a day when the thermometer reads 32°F., you will probably wear a coat, a hat, and gloves when you go outside. At zero degrees (0°F.) you will want to bundle up in a coat, hat, scarf, gloves, and a few sweaters. Any temperature below zero is even colder, and you would probably not want to go outside at all.

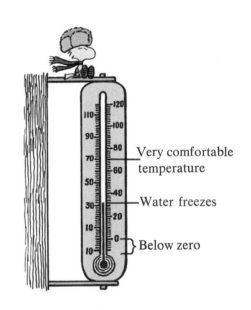

A Fahrenheit thermometer

## Are there any other thermometers besides Fahrenheit's?

Yes, there are a few more. One of these was invented by a man named Anders Celsius (SELL-see-us). On his thermometer, water freezes at zero degrees. We write this as 0°C. The "C." stands for Celsius. Water boils at 100°C. Those two numbers are easy to remember. That's probably why the Celsius thermometer is used almost all over the world.

# What place has the lowest temperature on record?

The place with the coldest temperature on record is near the South Pole. At a weather station called Vostok, 400 miles (640 kilometers) from the Pole, the temperature has gotten colder than 126 degrees below zero ($-126°$F., or $-88°$C.). No people live around the South Pole, except scientists who visit the weather station. But some people make their home in another very cold place—northern Siberia, in Asia. Temperatures there have gone down as low as 94 degrees below zero on the Fahrenheit thermometer ($-70°$ C.)!

# What place has the hottest temperature on record?

The hottest temperature ever recorded was in the country of Libya in North Africa. There, in one place in 1922, the temperature reached more than $136°$F. ($58°$C.)! If you look at the air thermometer in your house or school, you'll see that the numbers don't even go that high!

# Are deserts always hot?

No! Lucy may think that the promise "I will love you till the sands of the desert grow cold" means forever. But it really doesn't. The sands of deserts *do* grow cold, almost every night. The sun warms them during the day. But at night they can't keep their heat. In most places, moisture in the air acts like a blanket, holding the heat under it and keeping the earth warm at night. But air in the desert has less moisture in it than it does in most other places. So as soon as the sun disappears in the evening, the heat from the desert floor escapes into space.

413

## Why are deserts so dry?

Deserts are dry because they get very little rain. Many deserts are separated from the sea by mountains. Winds that blow onto the land from the sea carry a lot of moisture. When they start blowing up mountain slopes, these winds become cooler. Cooler winds cannot hold as much moisture as warmer ones. So the cooled-off winds drop their moisture in the form of rain or snow before reaching the mountaintops. By the time the winds reach the other side of the mountains, almost no moisture is left in them. The land on the other side of the mountains gets very little rain. It becomes a desert.

The Atacama Desert in Chile has had no rain for more than 400 years!

## Which place on earth gets the most rain?

A spot on the Hawaiian island of Kauai (kah-oo-AH-ee) gets about 460 inches (1,168 centimeters) of rain each year. That's at least 400 inches (1,016 centimeters) more than most other places in the United States. If you filled a long tube with 460 inches of rain, the water would rise as high as a four-story building!

414

# What makes the winds blow?

The air around us is always moving. It moves because the air temperature is different in different places. When air gets warmed by the sun, it gets lighter. It rises and then moves to a spot with colder air. The colder air sinks and then moves to the warm area. You feel this movement as wind.

There are two kinds of winds. One kind blows within a small area. For example, the air in a cloudy place is cooler than the air in a sunny place. The temperature difference causes the air to move, or the wind to blow.

The planetary (PLAN-ih-ter-ee) winds are the second kind of wind. They blow over large areas of the earth, and they blow all the time. Basically, they move between the cooler parts of the earth near the North Pole and South Pole and the warmer parts of the earth near the equator. Planetary winds move clouds and storms from one place in the world to another.

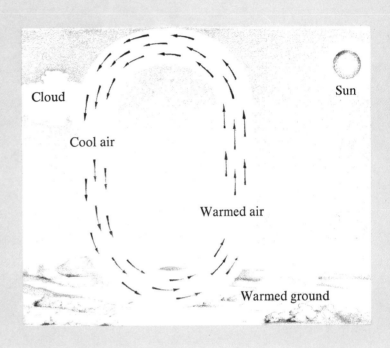

Cloud

Sun

Cool air

Warmed air

Warmed ground

# How fast can winds blow?

Near the ground, winds usually blow more slowly than a car on a highway—less than 50 miles (80 kilometers) an hour. High up in the air, winds blow faster. Wind speeds of up to 231 miles (370 kilometers) an hour have been measured at the top of Mt. Washington, in New Hampshire. That is about twice as fast as a taxicab could go if it were in a race. The fastest wind ever measured was in a tornado. It was moving at 280 miles (448 kilometers) an hour.

## What is a tornado?

A tornado is a noisy windstorm that often sweeps across parts of the United States. It looks like a long sleeve reaching down from a huge, dark cloud. In a tornado, wind whirls around and around in a circle about the size of two or three football fields. Very little air is in the center of this circle. Like a giant vacuum cleaner, the tornado can suck up anything in its path. Up go houses, cars, animals, people, and even railroad tracks. They may come down again later, far from where the storm picked them up. That's what happened to Dorothy and her dog, Toto, in *The Wizard of Oz*. A tornado can also flatten big buildings or even make them explode.

The whirling wind of a tornado can spin as fast as 280 miles (448 kilometers) an hour. But the whole tornado, spinning like a top, moves along at 20 to 40 miles (32 to 64 kilometers) an hour—about the speed of a car traveling down a city street.

416

# What is a hurricane?

A hurricane is a wild windstorm that starts at sea. Like a tornado, a hurricane is made up of whirling winds. But unlike a tornado, a hurricane is very large. It usually stretches across 300 or 400 miles (480 or 640 kilometers) at one time. These two pictures show the difference in size between a tornado and a hurricane.

Inside a hurricane, the wind is whirling at speeds of from 75 to 200 miles (120 to 320 kilometers) an hour. That's not quite as fast as the winds of a tornado, but it's fast all the same. A hurricane's wild winds cause huge waves to form on the ocean. The wind and waves can sink ships. They can tear up trees and buildings on islands and on mainland seashores. Hurricanes usually bring heavy rains, too. These rains, as well as the high waves, can cause great floods. People and animals are sometimes drowned in them.

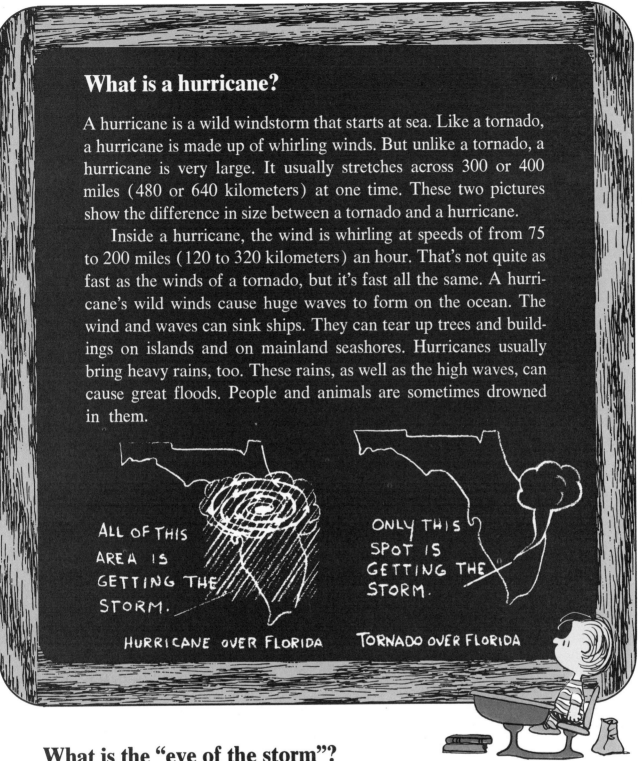

ALL OF THIS AREA IS GETTING THE STORM.

ONLY THIS SPOT IS GETTING THE STORM.

HURRICANE OVER FLORIDA

TORNADO OVER FLORIDA

# What is the "eye of the storm"?

At the center of a hurricane's circle of whirling winds is a quiet space with clear skies above. This is the "eye" of the hurricane. It is usually about 20 miles (32 kilometers) across. Some people think the hurricane is over when the "eye of the storm" reaches them. The wind dies down. The sky is bright above. But the whole storm circle is still traveling. Within a couple of hours the other side of the whirlwind will arrive. It will bring more wild winds and heavy rains.

417

## Where do puddles go when they dry up?

After a rain you usually see puddles in the street. A few hours later, the puddles are gone. What happened to them? They evaporated (ih-VAP-uh-rate-ed). This means that the water went up into the air and became part of it. When water is in this form we call it water vapor.

There is always some water vapor in the air. You cannot see it because it is in very tiny bits called particles (PAR-tih-kulz), which are scattered far apart from each other. The particles are so small that you could see them only under a microscope.

Water vapor comes from many places, not just from puddles. Water is always evaporating from hot pots over fires and from ponds, streams, rivers, lakes, and oceans.

## What is humidity?

Humidity is the moisture, or water vapor, in the air. If there is a lot of water vapor in the air, the humidity is high. If there is very little water vapor in the air, the humidity is low.

## What makes a cloud?

A cloud is made up of very tiny drops of water, called cloud droplets. Air always has some water vapor in it. If the air is warm, it is light, and it rises. As it rises it gets cooler. Cool air cannot hold as much water vapor as warm air. Particles of water vapor join together, or condense. They usually condense around tiny specks of dust or salt in the air. They form water droplets. If the air is very cold, they form bits of ice called ice crystals. The water droplets and ice crystals are light enough to float in the air. Any one droplet or ice crystal is too small for the eye to see. But a whole crowd of them make a cloud.

WHAT IS THIS, WHAT IS THIS... IS IT SMOG OR IS IT FOG?

YES!!

# What is fog?

A cloud that forms close to the ground is called fog. If you walk in fog, you cannot see separate little droplets, but you can often feel them on your face. A whole crowd of droplets can make such a thick fog cloud that you cannot see through it.

## What is smog?

The word "smog" is a combination of the words "smoke" and "fog." And that's pretty much what smog is.

The air always has some bits of dust floating around in it. In cities, other particles are also in the air—soot and smoke from chimneys, chemicals from factories, and fumes from automobile exhausts. We say such air is polluted. On breezy days, moving air carries the polluting particles away. On still days, a blanket of air heavy with moisture may hang over the city. Then none of the dirty particles blow away. Water droplets form around them. The cloud or fog they make is not colorless. It is dark. It is smog. When you breathe in a lot of the dirty particles all at once, they can hurt your lungs. Smog is the worst kind of air pollution.

OOPS...EXCUSE ME. I THOUGHT YOU WERE SNOOPY!

WEIRDO!!

EVEN IN A FOG, I FAIL TO SEE THE RESEMBLANCE!!

## Where does dew come from?

Dew is moisture from the air that has gathered in drops on leaves and blades of grass. During the day, the sun warms the earth. But at night, the earth and the air near it usually cool off. So do grasses and other plants. Cool air cannot hold as much moisture as warm air can. So some of the moisture in the air condenses into drops of water on the leaves and grass. These drops are dew.

## What is frost?

Frost is like dew. But when the night is very cold, the moisture in the air forms ice, or frost, instead of water, or dew. Like dew, frost forms on the grass and on other plants.

## Does "Jack Frost" really paint ferns on your window?

No. Jack Frost is a make-believe person. The ferns that appear on the inside of your window on cold nights are really ice crystals, or frost.

At night, before the "ferns" appear on the window, the glass is warm from the warm air inside your house. The air around the glass is warm, too. But then the outside temperature drops quickly below the freezing point. It makes the glass freezing cold. The freezing-cold glass cools the air next to your window, inside your house. The cooled air cannot hold as much water vapor as the warmer air. So the water vapor forms frost on the window. If the temperature of the window were above freezing, droplets of water like dew would form on the glass. It would become "steamed up."

# Why can you see your breath on a cold day?

If you go outside on a cold day and blow out your breath, you can see a small steamy cloud in the air. Your breath has moisture in it. Your breath is warm because the inside of your body is warm. When you blow that moist, warm breath into the cold out-of-doors air, your breath suddenly cools. Some of the moisture you have breathed out turns to water droplets. They form a small steamy cloud.

HEY, BIG SISTER... GOT NOTHING TO SAY? HAVE YOU LOST YOUR BREATH?

I'LL SHOW YOU BREATH!!! WHO MADE THAT SNOWWOMAN? WHO... WHO... WHO??!

## Where does rain come from?

Rain comes from clouds. When a cloud grows big, the cloud droplets in it begin to bump into one another. They join together and form big drops. The big drops are too heavy to float in the air. They fall to earth as rain.

IT'S RAINING CATS AND DOGS?! ...SOMETIMES WOODSTOCK'S EXPRESSIONS CAN GET PRETTY GROSS!

RAIN!

IT HELPS THINGS TO GROW... IT FILLS UP THE LAKES AND OCEANS SO THE FISH CAN SWIM AROUND AND IT GIVES US ALL SOMETHING TO DRINK...

WOODSTOCK DOESN'T CARE WHAT IT IS AS LONG AS HE UNDERSTANDS IT.

421

Raindrops are not tear shaped.
They are perfectly round!

## Why do we need rain?

At one time or another, we have all wanted the rain to go away and even to stay away. Rain can spoil a picnic or a ball game. But rain is very important to our lives.

Without rain, plants would die. They need water to live and grow. Animals, including people, would die, too. They would have no water to drink and no plants to eat. Nothing on earth could stay alive without rain.

AND NOW, HERE'S THE WORLD WAR I FLYING ACE LENDING HIS TALENTS TO MODERN SCIENCE.... SPRAYING CLOUDS WITH CHEMICALS TO MAKE RAIN. RAIN, YOU FOOL CLOUD.. RAIN... RAIN!!!

## Can people make rain fall?

People have made rain fall by spraying clouds with a chemical that helps raindrops form more quickly. Spraying clouds in this way is called "seeding." Seeding does not always work well. In dry lands where there are no clouds to spray, it cannot work at all.

Some people pray for rain or they do rain dances. Sometimes rain follows the dance or the prayers. But scientists don't believe that such methods really work.

# What causes thunderstorms?

We have thunderstorms when big, fluffy-looking clouds called thunderheads tower very high into the sky. They look beautiful when you see them at a distance. When the sun shines on their high-piled puffs, they look white. But as they sweep over your head and shut out the sunlight, they look very dark.

Thunderheads build up on hot, damp days when the very warm ground heats the moist air above it. The air rises higher and faster than usual. Water droplets gather into very big clouds. Some are several miles high! Inside each cloud, the warm rising air cools quickly. The cooled air sinks to a lower part of the thunderhead. There, the air is warmed again, and it rises. This rising and falling air makes violent winds inside the cloud. Large raindrops form. Lightning flashes, and thunder crashes.

# What is lightning?

Lightning is a flash of electricity in the air. There is electricity everywhere—in clouds, in the earth, even in you! Sometimes when you walk across a carpet and touch someone, you feel a tiny spark of electricity jump between the two of you.

In towering thunderclouds, a lot of electricity builds up. As clouds draw near to one another, huge sparks or flashes of electricity pass between two clouds. Or a flash may go from a cloud to the earth. The electricity heats the air along the path of the flash so much that the air glows. That glow is what we call lightning.

**!** Each second of every day about 100 bolts of lightning strike some part of the earth! **!**

# What is thunder?

When air is heated, the very tiny particles that make it up begin to move faster. The electrical flash from a thundercloud suddenly heats the air so much that all the particles move around wildly. The air shakes as huge numbers of them suddenly rush apart to get more space for their "dance." When this sudden huge movement in the air reaches our ears, we hear a thunderclap.

## Why do you see the lightning before you hear the thunder?

Light travels faster than you can imagine—186,282 miles (299,792 kilometers) in one second! So you see the glow of lightning the instant it flashes, even though it may be miles away. Sound travels much more slowly. It takes the sound of thunder nearly five seconds to travel one mile. So if a lightning flash is several miles away, you see the light right away. Then the sky darkens again. And after a pause you hear the thunder.

## How can you tell how far away lightning is?

Start counting as soon as you see a lightning flash. Count "one-Mississippi, two-Mississippi, three-Mississippi," and so on. Each number will take you about a second to say. Stop counting when you hear the thunderclap. That will give you the number of seconds the sound has taken to reach you. Allow five seconds for each mile (three seconds for a kilometer), and you can tell about how far away the lightning flash was. If you counted to "five-Mississippi," the flash was about a mile (a kilometer and a half) away. If you counted to ten, the flash was about two miles (three kilometers) away.

I DON'T BELIEVE HIM!!

# Can thunder and lightning hurt you?

Thunder can't hurt you, but lightning can. Thunder is just air shaking very hard. Lightning is electricity. A very small flash of electricity can give you a shock. A lightning flash is huge. It can burn whatever it touches, sometimes very badly.

Lightning usually strikes the highest thing around. This may be a skyscraper in a city, a tall tree in an open field, or a sailboat mast on the water. Metal lightning rods or specially wired television antennas can lead the electricity safely to the ground. They can keep a building safe from lightning damage. A metal car or airplane body can protect people inside it, too. However, if you stand under a big tree you will not be protected. The tree may be hit by the lightning, and the tree can fall on you. So if you are out in the open during a thunderstorm, you will be safest lying flat on the ground!

## What is hail?

Hail is made up of small lumps of ice that sometimes fall to earth during thunderstorms. These icy stones are formed inside the thunderclouds.

The tops of tall thunderhead clouds are always very cold. Down near the bottom of the clouds, the air is much warmer. Inside these clouds, warm air moves swiftly up and cold air moves swiftly down. Sometimes raindrops are blown up to the freezing-cold part of the cloud before they fall. There they turn to ice. Then they are blown down again and are coated with more raindrops. Before they fall to earth, the bits of ice may be blown up and down many times. Each time more raindrops gather on them and then freeze, to form extra layers of ice on the lump. Each lump of ice is called a hailstone. If many layers gather and freeze on one hailstone before it falls to the ground, it may grow quite large. Hailstones can break windows or dent car roofs. They can flatten plants in fields and gardens.

 Hailstones as big as your head have fallen. Some have measured 17 inches (43 centimeters) around. One weighed 1½ pounds (680 grams)!

## What is sleet?

Sleet is frozen rain. It falls when the air close to the ground is freezing cold. Sleet starts out as rain. As the raindrops fall, they freeze. They form the tiny ice balls known as sleet.

426

## What is an ice storm?

On some cold days, rain falls and turns to ice after it has landed. The frozen rain forms a smooth, slippery coat of ice on the freezing-cold street. We call this kind of rain freezing rain or an ice storm.

THINK OF IT THIS WAY... ONLY THREE MORE MONTHS TILL SPRING TRAINING.

## Is snow frozen rain?

No. Raindrops that freeze as they fall form sleet, not snow. Snowflakes are formed right in the clouds.

Clouds floating in freezing-cold air are made of tiny crystals of ice. As the air grows colder, more and more water vapor condenses around the ice. The tiny crystals grow bigger and bigger. The snowflakes you see are simply these crystals after they have grown too large and heavy to float in the air. They fall to earth as snow.

# What do snowflakes look like?

If you look at a group of snowflakes under a magnifying glass, you will see that they are like beautiful small lace doilies. They have many different sizes, shapes, and lovely patterns. However, if you count their sides, you will find that each of them has six. Each snowflake has six points, too.

No two snowflakes are exactly alike!

IT STAGGERS THE IMAGINATION...

JUST THINK..OUT OF THE BILLIONS AND BILLIONS OF SNOWFLAKES THAT HAVE FALLEN, NO TWO HAVE EVER BEEN ALIKE!

IT MAKES THE MIND REEL...

LUCY! LUCY! COME QUICK! I SAW THEM! I SAW THEM!

I SAW TWO SNOWFLAKES THAT WERE **EXACTLY** ALIKE!! COME QUICK!

THAT'S FUNNY...THEY WERE AROUND HERE SOMEWHERE..

SCHULZ

# Can you count all the snowflakes that fall?

Linus and Lucy say they have counted the snowflakes. This is a joke. No one could count all the snowflakes that fall. There are too many, and no one can see them all. Not Linus, not Lucy—not even you!

429

## How do the weather forecasters know what tomorrow's weather will be?

Tomorrow's weather is already building up in the air above the earth. Weather forecasters get reports on what is happening in the air all around the world. Many thousands of weather stations all around the world send out messages to weather forecasters. These stations measure the amount of rain or snow that falls in their area. They keep track of heat or cold with thermometers. They measure how heavy the air is, and how much moisture it holds. They find out how fast the planetary winds are carrying the weather and in what direction. Airlines and ships at sea send radio messages every few hours about the weather where they are. Cameras and other equipment circle the earth in weather satellites. They send back pictures and other information. All these facts are put together on special maps. The maps show what kind of weather is heading your way, wherever you are.

430

# What are cold fronts and warm fronts?

A cold front is the leading edge of a moving clump of cold air called a cold air mass. An air mass is a large blob of air that stays together as it moves across the earth. The entire blob has about the same amount of moisture and temperature. Its temperature and moisture depend on where it comes from. A cold front often brings showers and thunderstorms with fast winds.

A warm front is the leading edge of a warm air mass. It often brings along steady rains or snow.

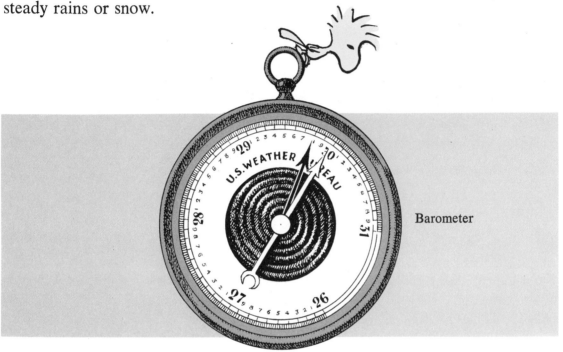

Barometer

# What do weather forecasters mean when they say the barometer is rising?

In a weather report the weather forecaster may say that the barometer (buh-ROM-uh-tur) is rising or falling. A barometer is a special instrument that measures how heavily the air is pressing on the earth. When the barometer is rising, it means that the air is pressing harder and harder on the earth. When the barometer is falling, it means that the air is pressing less and less on the earth.

Knowing the air pressure helps people predict the weather. When the air pressure is rising, clear skies and cool weather are probably on their way. When the air pressure is falling, stormy weather is probably in store for us.

The word "High," circled on a weather map, shows the center of high air pressure. The word "Low," circled on a weather map, shows the center of low air pressure.

# What good are weather forecasts?

Weather forecasts tell what weather is coming. They help people know what kind of clothes to wear. They warn farmers against frosts that might ruin their crops. Weather forecasts warn people along seacoasts against hurricanes, and in other places against tornadoes, so they can close up their homes and get to safe shelters. In the winter, forecasts tell skiers how much snow will fall. During the summer they tell people how warm and sunny the beaches will be. They warn when smog will be bad in cities. They say when roads will be slippery or foggy and dangerous for driving. They help airplane pilots choose safe routes to fly.

Unfortunately, the weather doesn't always work out the way it's been forecast. Winds sometimes change direction. They blow storm clouds to unexpected places. Sometimes winds speed up or slow down. Then weather changes reach an area later or sooner than forecast. Nevertheless, the weather forecasters do a lot to help people keep comfortable and safe.

# Did You Know That...

When it's daylight on one side of the earth, it's dark on the other side. While you are watching the sun rise on one side, the people on the other side are watching it set. The world has 24 different time zones—one for each hour of the day. If it is noon on Sunday in Los Angeles, it's three in the afternoon in New York and nine in the evening in Paris. And in Tokyo, it's already five o'clock Monday morning.

LOS ANGELES   NEW YORK   PARIS   TOKYO

SUN.    SUN.    SUN.    MON.

The earth is not perfectly round! It bulges slightly around the middle. The distance around the earth at the equator is 85 miles more than the distance around the earth from pole to pole.

The earth is surrounded by a layer of air called atmosphere (AT-muss-fear). Most of the atmosphere is within 20 miles of the earth's surface. But the layer reaches as high as 600 miles. Even though the atmosphere is invisible, it's very important. The air we breathe is part of it. Our weather comes from it. The atmosphere helps keep the sun's heat close to the earth's surface, and it screens out the kinds of sunlight that can be harmful to us.

Auroras (ah-ROR-uhz) are like a light show in the atmosphere. Particles from the sun crash into particles of the atmosphere miles above the earth and these collisions produce a glow that forms the aurora. Most auroras can only be seen near the North and South Poles. The most famous aurora is in the Northern Hemisphere, the Aurora Borealis.

At the North Pole daylight lasts all spring and summer. In fact, the sun shines 24 hours a day for six straight months. When the sun finally does set at the beginning of autumn, it doesn't return again for half a year. The North Pole is in darkness all fall and winter!

Each country of the world has its own flag. The 50 stars of the American flag stand for the 50 states; the 13 stripes stand for the original 13 states. The red cross in the center of the British flag represents St. George of England, the diagonal white cross represents St. Andrew of Scotland, and the diagonal red cross represents St. Patrick of Northern Ireland. The flag of the African country of Gabon has three stripes. The green stripe stands for the forests, the yellow stripe for the sun, and the blue stripe for the sea.

Flag of Gabon

Flag of the United Kingdom